MATH GRADE 2
WARM-UPS

Developing Fluency In Math

Written by **Sheri Disbrow**   Illustrated by **Stephanie O'Shaughnessy**

Prufrock Press Inc.
P.O. Box 8813
Waco, TX 76714-8813
Phone: (800) 998-2208
Fax: (800) 240-0333
http://www.prufrock.com

Introduction

Do You Need Another Math Book?

If you already use a basal text, do you really need another math book? For most teachers, the answer is "yes." This supplementary math book reinforces the concepts presented in basal texts, giving additional, consistent review of the most important math concepts that are presented at this grade level. Even teachers who use a basal text will find it necessary to give additional practice to assure that students have a concrete grasp of mathematical concepts. *Math Warm-Ups* is challenging and integrates a variety of content in each lesson. It gradually increases in difficulty, making it the perfect math supplement.

Math Warm-Ups and Math Standards

This is one in a series of supplementary math text books. Each book is a daily math workbook, designed to meet math standards for a specific grade level. This book was developed according to the national, Ohio, California, and Texas content standards and objectives for second grade.

Each page of *Math Warm-Ups* offers ten problems that deal with a variety of concepts. The problems address the following math standards:

♦ understand the meaning of addition and subtraction
♦ compute fluently and make estimates
♦ recognize and extend patterns
♦ name and draw two- and three-dimensional shapes
♦ apply transformation
♦ measure using various units or systems
♦ represent data in pictures and graphs
♦ analyze data
♦ apply appropriate strategies to solve problems
♦ use the language of mathematics to express mathematical ideas.

What's So Great About This Book?

This book consistently exposes students to a variety of concepts in all objective areas including common sense. It is quick and easy for the teacher to grade and provides immediate and repeated opportunities for re-teaching. *Math Warm-Ups* is designed to aid the teacher in covering all objectives and provides the students with opportunities to practice several math objectives within a five day period. It stimulates learning and encourages the use of different problem solving techniques. The advantages of using this text are that it:

♦ is easy to grade
♦ motivates students
♦ provides daily diagnosis of students' weaknesses
♦ covers a variety of objectives
♦ spirals in level of difficulty
♦ consistently builds critical thinking and problem solving skills
♦ addresses problem solving daily in small pieces
♦ combines multiple objectives into several questions
♦ presents multi-step problems
♦ asks open ended questions
♦ provides practice with analogies
♦ supports the existing curriculum
♦ eliminates "holes" in learning, thus enabling students to meet standards
♦ can be used individually or with a whole class
♦ provides a quick diagnosis of new students' abilities
♦ addresses all objectives within a five-day period
♦ enables productive parent conferences, pinpointing problem areas
♦ assists teachers in finding weak areas where additional instructional focus is needed.

How to Use the Book

This workbook is can be used in a variety of ways. It can be used as a warm-up, as homework, or as a diagnostic tool. You can use it as a daily or weekly review or as additional practice to supplement your regular math instruction.

Teachers, parents, and administrators can use this workbook to diagnose weak areas and assure the conceptual understanding of the students on a daily basis. Parents, students, and teachers can evaluate progress which will allow them to identify and correct deficiencies. It empowers students and motivates them to invest in their own learning. Parents who want to make sure that their children have mastered math skills and will be ready for any testing situation will find this workbook thorough and easy to use. Additionally, teachers who want to provide individual practice for students who are ready to move faster through the curriculum can use these exercises and be comfortable that students are getting practice in a broad spectrum of math skills.

The **Math Warm-Ups** series came out of a need to ensure students' success while developing mathematical thinkers and problem solvers. It has been tested and used in the classroom with great success. Students who use these exercises are interested and motivated because they are given repeated opportunities to be successful. Practicing annual expectations and goals on a daily basis, builds student self-esteem and confidence, while improving attitudes and grades. Enjoy the book and the rewards that come with it.

Exercise 1

1. Sam had 8 cookies. He gave 2 cookies to his sister. How many cookies did Sam have left?

Sam has ____ cookies left.

2. Count the money.

_____ ¢

3. Complete the pattern.

5, 10, 15, ____, 25, _____

The rule is _____

_____

4. Write the numeral for this word.

seventeen _____

5. Is 6 even or odd?

Six is _____.

6. About how long is the pencil?

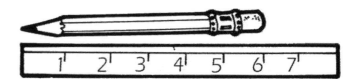

_____ units

7. What time is shown on the clock?

____ : ____

8. Circle the one's place in this number

852

9. Write this numeral:

300 + 60 + 7 = _____

10. Circle the second clock.

🕰 🕰 🕰 🕰 🕰 🕰 🕰

1. Bianca has three books. Chris has five books. His favorite book is about animals. How many more books does Chris have than Bianca?

_____ more

2. What time is shown on the clock?

____ : ____

6. Complete the analogy.

7.
```
  12          212
 + 5         + 50
 ___         ____
```

3. Shade $\frac{1}{2}$ of this candy bar.

candy

8.
```
  13          130
 - 7         - 70
 ___         ____
```

4. Continue the pattern.

3, 5, 7, ____, ____, ____

The rule is _____

5. Give two reasons why this is a square.

_____

_____

9. ____ + 3 = 5

10. Complete the fact family.

2 + 3 = ____

____ + ____ = ____

5 − ____ = ____

____ − ____ = ____

Exercise 3

1. What time is shown on the clock?

____ : ____

....

2. Shade half of this pizza.

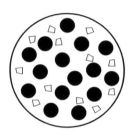

....

3. Continue the pattern.

11, 13, 15, ____, ____, ____

....

4. Circle the even numbers.

1 2 3 4 5 6 7

....

5. Continue the pattern by adding three more shapes.

6. Jill poured one cup of juice in a pitcher. Then she poured two more cups of juice in the pitcher. Shade the pitcher to show how many cups of juice are in the pitcher now.

....

7. How much money is shown?

_____ cents

....

8. 6   7
     +6   +7

....

9. 8   9
     +8   +9

....

10. 2 dimes = _____ cents

Exercise 4

Name _____

1. Dora had 12 candy kisses. She gave 9 to her friend. How many candy kisses does Dora have left?

Dora has _____ candy kisses left.

2. Complete the analogy.

four : two :: eight : _____

4 : 2 :: 8 : _____

3. What is the total of the coins shown below?

_____ cents

4. Circle the tens digit in this number.

682

5. What time is shown on the clock?

____ : ____

6. Divide this rectangle into four equal parts. Label each part $\frac{1}{4}$.

7.
16	16	16
+2	− 2	+16

8.
12	12	22
− 8	+ 8	+ 8

9. About how much does your math book weigh?

1 pound   1 ounce   10 pounds

10. Continue the pattern.

12, 14, 16, ____, ____, ____

The rule is _____

Exercise 5

Use the graph to answer questions 1, 2, and 3.

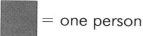

Favorite Colors

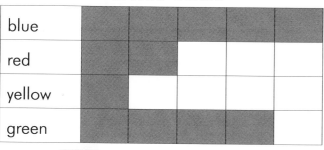

blue					
red					
yellow					
green					

▓ = one person

1. How many people like the color blue the best? _____

2. How many people like the color green the best? _____

3. What is the least favorite color?

_____

4. Complete the analogy.

weight : pounds :: length : ___

a. ton   **b.** pints   **c.** feet

5. What time is shown on the clock?

____ : ____

6.   7   7
        −3   −4

7.   4   14
        +3   +3

8. Circle the two things that are same.

9. What shape is this?

_____

10. January is the _____ month of the year.

a. third   **b.** first   **c.** twelfth

Exercise 6

1. Samantha has 10 ribbons in her drawer. Two of the ribbons are white and 8 of the ribbons are blue. If she reaches into her drawer without looking, what color will she be more likely to pull out?

She will be more likely to pull out a _____ ribbon out of the drawer.

2. Circle the name of this coin.

nickel

dime

quarter

Two of these coins equals _____ ¢

3. A nickel is worth _____ ¢

4. Finish and fact family.

7 + ____ = 10

3 + 7 = ____

10 − 7 = ____

10 − ____ = 7

5. Finish the pattern.

5, 7, 9, ___, ___, ___

6. Circle the hundreds digit in this number.

2 0 2

7. Color half of the faces.

Write a fraction for the number you colored.

$$\frac{}{2} \quad \text{or} \quad \frac{}{10}$$

8. Circle the fifth cake.

9. Is the number 8 even or odd?

The number 8 is _____

10. Complete the analogy.

2 : 4 :: 3 : ___

a. 13   **b.** 9   **c.** 6

Exercise 7

1. Troy ate 3 doughnuts. Then he ate 6 more doughnuts. How many doughnuts did Troy eat in all?

_____ doughnuts altogether

2. What time is shown on the clock?

____ : ____

3. Complete the analogy.

a.m. : before noon :: p.m. : ____

a. after noon   b. time   c. noon

4. Continue counting by fives.

35, 40, 45, ____, ____, ____

5. About how much would an apple weigh?

6 ounces   6 pounds   600 pounds

6. Put these numbers in order from least to greatest.

9 10 4 5 8 6

____ ____ ____ ____ ____ ____

7. How much money is shown?

_____ ¢

8. 12   3
      + 3   +12

9. If the answer is 6, what is the problem? Circle one problem.

11   11   11   5
+5   −6   −5   +6

10. About how tall are you?

1 meter   1 centimeter

Exercise 8

1. Joey had 10 strawberries. He gave half of them to his sister. How many strawberries did Joey have? _____

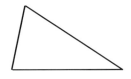

How many strawberries does Joey's sister have? _____

2. What time is shown on the clock?

____ : ____

3. Divide this circle into 4 equal pieces. Label each part 1/4.

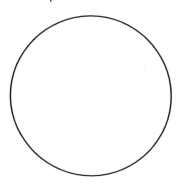

4. What month comes after March?

_____

5. What number comes between?

27 _____ 29

6. Complete the analogy.

square : 4 :: triangle : ___

a. 6   **b.** 3   **c.** 90°

7. What is the name of this shape?

_____

8. 18   18   180
       +1   −1   −10
       ___   ___   ___

9. How many different ways can you complete this number sentence?

___ + ___ = 10   ___ + ___ = 10

___ + ___ = 10   ___ + ___ = 10

___ + ___ = 10   ___ + ___ = 10

___ + ___ = 10   ___ + ___ = 10

10. How many tens are in this number?

321

There are _____ tens.

Exercise 9

Use this chart to answer questions 1 and 2.

Weather This Week

rainy			
sunny	☼	☼	☼
cloudy	☁	☁	☁

each square = 1 day

1. How many sunny days were there in the week?

_____ days

2. How many more sunny days were there than rainy days in the week?

_____ days

3. What time is shown on the clock?

_____ : _____

4. Complete the analogy

pentagon : 5 :: square : ___

a. 4   **b.** rectangle   **c.** 8

5. 2 nickels = _____ dime

4 nickels = _____ dimes

6. Insert <, =, or > to make this a true number sentence.

18 ⬭ 11

7. Fill in the missing numbers.

91, 90, ____, ____, ____, 86

The rule is _____

8. Circle the ones digit in this number.

548

9. 16 – ____ = 2

10.
$$\begin{array}{cccc} 6 & 6 & 7 & 7 \\ +6 & +7 & +7 & +8 \\ \hline \end{array}$$

Name _____

1. James had 15 cents. His brother gave him 16 pennies. How much money does James have now?

James has _____ cents.

2. Julie has 1 dime and 1 penny. James has 3 nickels. Who has more money James or Julie? How much more?

_____   _____

3. Complete the analogy.

dime : 10 :: quarter : _____

4. _____ pennies = 1 dime

_____ pennies = 2 dimes

_____ pennies = 3 dimes

5.

10	10	10	10
−1	−2	−3	−4

6. Divide these airplanes into 2 equal groups.

7. Complete the pattern.

15, 20, 25, ____, ____

8. The cats are lined up by color. The first, third, and sixth cats are orange. The rest of the cats are yellow. Circle the orange cats.

9.

11	12
−5	−6

10. If 10 is the answer, what is the problem? Circle one.

4 + 7   20 − 5

4 + 6   6 + 6

Exercise 11

Use this chart to answer
questions 1 and 2.

Color of Socks in Our Class

white	/ / / / /
black	/ / / /
brown	/ / /

/ = 1 pair of socks

1. How many students are in this class?

_____ students

2. What color of socks are the least
number of students wearing?

_____

3. Complete the analogy.

clock : hour :: calendar : _____

a. time   **b.** months   **c.** minutes

4. _____ pennies = 1 nickel

_____ pennies = 2 nickels

_____ pennies = 3 nickels

5. Write the numerals for these words.

five _____

eleven _____

6. Circle the even numbers.

2 3 4 5 6 7

7. What time will it be
in half an hour from
the time shown on
the clock?

____ : ____

8. Shade half of this figure.

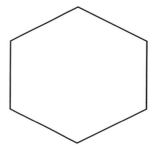

9. ____ + 4 = 8

8 − 4 = ____

10. 12   12   22
       −3   +3   +3

Exercise 12

Name _____

1. Jackie has sixteen cans of soda. She wants to share them equally with her friend Maggie. How many cans of soda will each of them get?

Maggie will get _____ sodas.

Jackie will get _____ sodas.

2. What time is shown on the clock?

_____ : _____

3. Complete the analogy.

 : :: : _____

a. ⬡ 　 b. ⬡ 　 c. ⬡

The relationship is _____

_____

4. This shape is a _____.

5. About how tall is a door in your classroom?

7 feet 　 7 inches 　 7 miles

6. Finish these number sentences for the number family 6, 2, 8.

6 + 2 = _____

2 + _____ = _____

8 – _____ = _____

8 – _____ = _____

7. _____ minutes = 1 hour

_____ minutes = 1/2 hour

8. _____ nickels = 1 dime

_____ nickels = 2 dimes

_____ nickels = 3 dimes

9. _____ + 7 = 20

20 – 7 = _____

10.
$$\begin{array}{r} 13 \\ -5 \\ \hline \end{array} \qquad \begin{array}{r} 5 \\ + \\ \hline 13 \end{array} \qquad \begin{array}{r} 7 \\ 3 \\ +5 \\ \hline \end{array}$$

Exercise 13

1. Harry had 10 toy snakes. 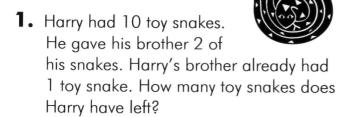 He gave his brother 2 of his snakes. Harry's brother already had 1 toy snake. How many toy snakes does Harry have left?

Harry has _____ snakes left.

2. How much time is between the time shown on the clock and 2:10?

____ hour and ____ minutes

3. How much money is shown?

_____ ¢

4. What is the difference between a rectangle and a square:

_____

_____

_____

5. Circle the tens digit in this number.

41

6. Insert >, =, or < to make this a true number sentence.

16 ◯ 15 + 1

7. Write numerals for these words.

six _____

seventeen _____

eighty-nine_____

8. ____ quarter = 25¢

half dollar = ____ ¢

9. ____ + 5 = 17

5 + 17 = ____

10. 13   14   15
      −7   −7   −7

How does knowing 7 + 7 = 14 help with these problems? _____

_____

Exercise 14

1. Mario's mom gives him 10¢ for every A on his report card. He got four A's and two B's.
How much money will Mario get?

Mario will get ____ ¢.

2. Draw hands on the clock to show 8:15.

3. Complete the analogy.

$\frac{1}{4}$: quarter :: $\frac{1}{2}$: ___

a. half   **b.** double   **c.** second

4. _____ pennies = 1 quarter

_____ pennies = 2 quarter

_____ pennies = 3 quarter

5. Insert >, =, or < to make this a true number sentence.

26 ◯ 29

6. Finish the pattern.

88, 89, ____, ____, ____

The rule is _____

7. Circle the odd numbers.

4 5 6 7 8 9 10 11 12

Use any of the odd numbers to write two number sentences that have a sum of 20.

_____

_____

8. Shade 1/2 of this circle and write a fraction to show the shaded part.

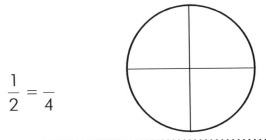

$\frac{1}{2} = \frac{}{4}$

9. If the answer is 19, what is the question? Circle the problem.

$\begin{array}{c} 14 \\ +7 \\ \hline \end{array}$ $\begin{array}{c} 13 \\ +6 \\ \hline \end{array}$ $\begin{array}{c} 13 \\ +7 \\ \hline \end{array}$

10. 140 − 80 = _____

Exercise 15

1. Cara has 6 shelves in her bookcase. She puts 1 doll on the first shelf, 2 dolls on the second shelf, and 3 on the third shelf. Continuing this pattern, how many dolls will be on the fifth shelf?

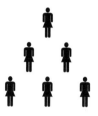

_____ dolls

2. Complete the analogy.

12 : 6 :: 6 : ___

a. six   **b.** 3   **c.** 2

3. Draw hands on the clock to show 3:30.

4. About how long is a second grader's foot?

2 feet   7 inches   1 inch

5. Circle the seventh apple.

6. Continue the pattern.

25, 30, 35, ____, ____, ____

The rule is _____

7. Color half of this circle and write a fraction to show the shaded part.

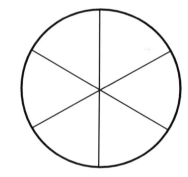

$\frac{1}{2} = \frac{}{6}$

8. 1 quarter = _____ cents

1 quarter + 1 nickel = _____ cents

1 quarter + 1 dime = _____ cents

9. ____ + 6 = 24

10.

$$\begin{array}{cc} 12 \\ -6 \\ \hline \end{array} \quad \begin{array}{c} \\ +6 \\ \hline 12 \end{array} \quad \begin{array}{c} 13 \\ -6 \\ \hline \end{array} \quad \begin{array}{c} \\ +6 \\ \hline 13 \end{array}$$

Exercise 16

1. Steven wants to see a  movie about sharks. The movie starts at 3:00 p.m. It lasts an hour and a half. Will he get out in time to meet his friend at 5:00 p.m.?

_____

2. Draw lines to connect equal numbers.

10 tens   400

40 tens   700

70 tens   100

3. How much money is shown?

_____ cents

4. Insert >, =, or < to make this a true number sentence.

16 ◯ 11

5. Finish the fact family for 7, 4 and 11.

7 + ___ = 11   11 − ___ = ___

___ + ___ = 11   11 − ___ = ___

6. Write three 2-digit numbers that have even numbers in the ten's place.

_____   _____   _____

7. Circle the odd numbers.

16   17   18   19   20

Find the sum of the odd numbers.

___ + ___ = _____

8. Circle the triangle.

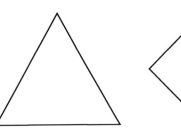 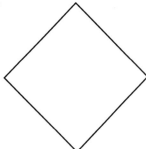

9. If the answer is 10, which of these could be the problem? Circle one.

11 − 3   5 + 7

8 + 2   15 − 3

10. Write the value of three coins so that they are equal to 25¢

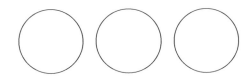

Exercise 17

Name _____

1. Randy had 20¢. He bought a pencil for 15¢. How much money does Randy have now?

Randy has _____ ¢

2. What time is shown on the clock?

____ : ____

3. Complete the analogy.

yesterday : today :: today : _____

a. morning   **b.** tonight   **c.** tomorrow

4. Put these numbers in order from least to greatest.

48   49   46   44   45

____ ____ ____ ____ ____

5. What month comes after September?

_____

6. How much money is shown ?

_____ ¢

7. Circle the even numbers.

1 2 12 13 20

Use the even numbers to write a subtraction problem that has the largest difference.

_____

8.
$$\begin{array}{cc} 2 & 7 \\ 4 & 3 \\ +2 & +6 \end{array}$$

9. Circle the square.

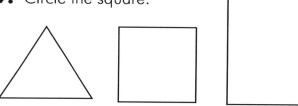

10. 16 − 8 = ___

17 − 8 = ___

18 − 8 = ___

Exercise 18

Use this graph to answer questions 1 and 2.

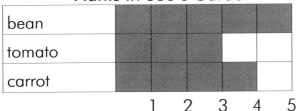

Plants in Sue's Garden

1. How many bean plants is Sue growing?

_____ bean plants.

2. What plant does Sue have the least of?

Sue has the least _____ plants.

....

3. Complete the analogy.

Saturday : Sunday :: Sunday : ____

a. Monday **b.** church **c.** school

....

4. Count on by tens.

20, 30, ____, ____, ____, ____

....

5. Circle the picture that shows $\frac{1}{6}$.

6. Finish the problems for the fact family 6, 8, 14.

___ + ___ = 14

14 – ___ = ___

___ + ___ = 14

14 – ___ = ___

....

7. Circle the hundreds digit in this number.

6 3 4

Write the number that is 1 less than this number.

_____

....

8. How much money is shown?

_____ ¢

....

9. 5 + 2 + 15 = ____

....

10. If the answer is 10, which of these could be the problem? Circle one.

16	16	10
−10	−6	+6

Exercise 19

1. Jane had 15 hats. Her dad bought her 9 more hats. How many hats did Jane have then?

Jane had _____ hats.

2. What time is shown on the clock?

____ : ____

How many minutes until 5 o'clock?

_____ minutes

3. Complete the analogy.

eggs : dozen :: gloves : _____

a. pair   **b.** hand   **c.** warm

4. Circle the odd numbers and put them in order from greatest to least.

5   1   3   2   7   6   4

_____

5. Insert >, =, or < to make this a true number sentence.

100 ⬭ 500

6. Circle $\frac{1}{3}$ of the ice cream cones.

7. How many cents is this?

_____ ¢

8. Finish the pattern.

3, 6, 9, ____, ____, ____

9. Complete the fact family.

4 + 8 = ____

____ + 4 = ____

8 − 4 = ____

____ + 4 = ____

10.
```
 18        18        18
 −2        −3        −4
___       ___       ___
```

Exercise 20

1. Tracy the turtle was first in line. Pat the penguin was behind Randy the rabbit. Write each name to show how they were lined up.

_____   _____   _____
  first   second   third

2. How many minutes until the next hour?

____ minutes

What time will it be then?

____ : ____

3. Shade 3/5 the pentagon

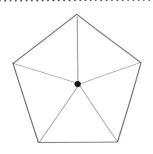

4. Count on by tens.

43, 53, ____, ____, ____, ____

5. Jude's birthday is January 3rd. Tracy's birthday is May 3rd. How many months between the two friends' birthdays?

____ months

6. Continue the pattern

89, 88, 87, ____, ____, ____

7. How much money is shown?

_____ ¢

8. 7 tens + 6 ones = ____

9. Use the numbers 3, 2, 6, and 9 to make the largest 4-digit number you can.

_____

10.
28	27	26
−4	−4	−4

Exercise 21

Name _____

Use this calendar for questions 1, 2, 3 and 4.

Sun	Mon	Tues	Wed	Thurs	Fri	Sat
				1	2	3
4	5	6	7	8	9	10
11	12	13	14	15	16	17
18	19	20	21	22	23	24
25	26	27	28	29	30	31

1. There are _____ Saturdays in this month.

2. The third Monday is on the _____ th day .

3. Play practice is every Monday, Wednesday and Friday beginning the first Monday. The last practice is on the 19th. How many days of play practice are there?

_____ days

4. The costumes for the play arrive on the morning of the second Friday. For how many practices can the actors use the costumes?

_____ practices

5. Complete the pattern.

▲■◆◆▲■◆◆ ___ ___ ___ ___

6. Put these numbers in order from least to greatest.

35 25 15 45 55

_____

7. Shade the last two figures to complete the pattern.

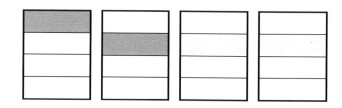

8. Circle a third of the snakes and write a fraction that shows the circled part.

🐍 🐍 🐍 🐍 🐍 🐍
🐍 🐍 🐍 🐍 🐍 🐍

$$\frac{1}{3} = \frac{}{12}$$

9. $4 + 17 =$ _____

$17 + 4 =$ _____

10. What would you use to measure sugar for making a batch of cookies?

a. gallon   b. cup   c. quart

Exercise 22

Name _____

1. Mrs. Kim bought 7 loaves of wheat bread and 2 loaves of white bread. How many more loaves of wheat bread did she buy?

_____ more loaves

Each loaf has 20 slices. How many slices of white bread does she have?

_____ slices of white bread.

2. Draw hands on the clock to show 3:30.

3. Use all of the numbers **4, 8, 2,** and **1** to make the smallest number possible.

_____

4. Count on by fives.

25, 30, ____, ____, ____

5. 1 week = ____ days

2 weeks = ____ days

1 year = ____ months

6. Complete the pattern

1, 3, 5, 7, 9, ____, ____, ____

The rule is _____

7. Circle the cylinder.

8. How much money would you have if you had a dime more than the amount shown?

_____ ¢

9.
$$\begin{array}{r} 34 \\ -\ 4 \\ \hline \end{array} \qquad \begin{array}{r} 34 \\ +\ 4 \\ \hline \end{array}$$

10.
$$\begin{array}{r} 23 \\ -2 \\ \hline \end{array} \qquad \begin{array}{r} 22 \\ -2 \\ \hline \end{array} \qquad \begin{array}{r} 21 \\ -2 \\ \hline \end{array}$$

Exercise 23

1. Lucy caught 2 fish before lunch and 6 fish after lunch. Miguel only caught 1 fish. How many fish did Lucy and Miguel catch in all?

Miguel and Lucy caught _____ fish.

2. About how long is this ribbon?

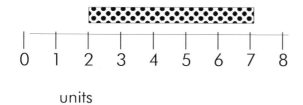

_____ units

3. Complete the analogy.

   : _____

a.   b.   c.

4. Continue the pattern.

91, 81, 71, ____, ____, ____

5. How much money is shown?

_____ ¢

6. Circle the **odd** numbers and find the sum of these numbers.

9 10 11 12 13

____ + ____ + ____ = ____ .

7. Write the names for these shapes.

_____   _____

8. Circle one fifth of the trucks. Write a fraction for the circled part.

$$\frac{1}{5} = \frac{}{10}$$

9. If the answer is 19, which of these could be the problem? Circle the correct problem.

a. 14 + 6

b. 13 + 6

c. 12 + 8

10.   63   63
         −3   +3
       ____   ____

Exercise 24

Use this graph to answer questions 1, 2, and 3.

Favorite Breakfast Foods

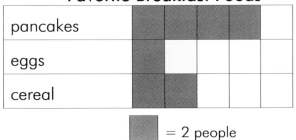

pancakes					
eggs					
cereal					

▨ = 2 people

1. How many people like pancakes best?

_____

2. How many people like eggs best?

_____

3. How many more people like pancakes than people who like eggs?

_____

4. Count on by tens.

25, 35, 45, ____, ____, ____

5. Complete this figure to make it symmetrical.

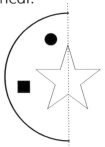

6. Insert >, =, or < to make this a true number sentence.

76 ◯ 67

7. Complete the patterns.

1, ____, ____, 4, 5, 6

I, ____, ____, IV, V, VI

8. Soccer practice is at 9:00. How much time before practice starts?

_____ minutes

9.
```
  2        6
  3        2
+7       +4
```

10.
```
 11       11       11
 -1       -2       -3
```

Exercise 25

1. Mary has 6 balloons. Three of them are white. Jack has 8 balloons. Together how many balloons do Mary and Jack have?

_____ balloons altogether

If they divide the balloons evenly between them, how many balloons will each person get?

_____ balloons each

2. Complete the analogy.

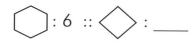

3. Draw hands on the clock to show 3:45.

4. About how long is this bracelet?

_____ units

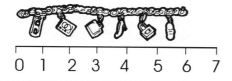

5. Name this shape.

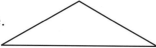

_____

How many sides does it have? _____

6. Complete this pattern.

199, 198, _____, 196, _____, 194

This rule is _____

7. What are all the even numbers between 10 and 20?

_____

8. Circle $\frac{1}{5}$ of these stars.

9. $\begin{array}{r} 6 \\ +2 \\ \hline \end{array}$ $\begin{array}{r} 2 \\ +6 \\ \hline \end{array}$ $2 + 6 = 6 +$ _____

10. There are 20 people in our class. Half of the people eat sandwiches for lunch.
How many people eat sandwiches?

_____ people

Exercise 26

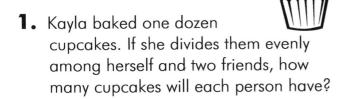

Name _____

1. Kayla baked one dozen cupcakes. If she divides them evenly among herself and two friends, how many cupcakes will each person have?

They will each have _____ cupcakes.

2. What time is shown on the clock?

____ : ____

3. Complete the analogy.

3 : 6 :: 5 : ____

a. 10   **b.** 8   **c.** 15

4. Put these numbers in order from greatest to least.

13   11   17   15   19

____   ____   ____   ____   ____

5. Write the numerals for these numbers.

four = _____

fourteen = _____

forty = _____

6. About how long should it take to eat dinner?

30 minutes   3 hours   3 days

7. How much money is shown?

_____ ¢

Show one other way to make the same amount of money using 5 coins.

8. Draw a line of symmetry for each polygon.

9.
14	4	24
+6	+6	+6

10.
31	44	28	67
−10	−10	−10	−10

Exercise 27

1. There are 12 boys and 8 girls on the school bus. How many children are on the school bus?

_____ children on the bus

If 12 more girls get on and 3 boys get off the bus, how many children will be on the bus?

_____ children on the bus.

2. What time is shown on the clock?

____ : ____

3. Complete the analogy.

3 : 6 :: 4 : _____

a. 8   **b.** 5   **c.** 12

4. Count on by tens.

15, 25, ____, ____, ____, ____

5. Write the fractions for the **shaded** part of each picture.

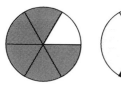

_____   _____   _____

6. Finish the fact family 7, 8, 15.

____ + ____ = 15

15 − ____ = ____

____ + ____ = ____

15 − ____ = ____

7. How much money is shown?

_____ ¢

8. Insert >, =, or < to make this a true number sentence.

43 ◯ 34

9.
```
  6        5
  3        4
 +3       +3
```

10.
```
 38      38      38
 -6      -7      -8
```

Exercise 28

Name _____

1. There were 19 geese on the lake. Seven geese flew away. How many geese are still on the lake?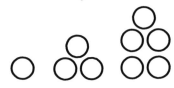

_____ geese left

Half the geese that are left are males. How many of the geese are females?

_____ female geese

2. Draw hands on the clock to show 12:45.

3. Shade each shape to show the fraction below the circle.

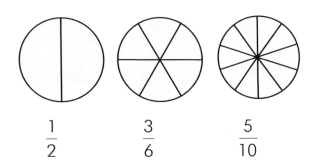

$\dfrac{1}{2}$ $\dfrac{3}{6}$ $\dfrac{5}{10}$

4. Put these numbers in order from greatest to least.

235 215 225 230 220

_____ _____ _____ _____ _____

5. Complete the pattern by adding two more figures.

6. On the line by each number write whether it is odd or even.

10 _____   15 _____

25 _____   30 _____

7. Write the number equal to:

2 thousands + 1 hundred + 6 tens + 2 ones

_____

8. What month is two months after April?

_____

9.
$\begin{array}{r} 42 \\ +12 \\ \hline \end{array}$ $\begin{array}{r} 43 \\ +12 \\ \hline \end{array}$ $\begin{array}{r} 143 \\ +12 \\ \hline \end{array}$

10. Use the numbers 10, 30, 40, 60, 70, and 90 to make number sentences.

_____ + _____ = 100

_____ + _____ = 100

_____ + _____ = 100

Exercise 29

1. Juan, Chris, and Tim were eating cake. Juan and Chris each ate two pieces. Tim only ate one piece. How many total pieces of cake did all three of them eat?

The boys ate _____ pieces of cake.

2. It takes 10 minutes to wash his bike. What time did Bryce start if he finished at 10:15 a.m.?

_____ : _____

3. Complete the analogy.

☐ : ■ :: △ :

4. Count on by fives.

30, 35, ____, ____, ____

5. Shade $\frac{1}{3}$ of the cats.

6. Continue the pattern.

199, 198, 197, ____, ____, ____

7. Circle the fifth watering can in the second row.

8. What would the temperature most likely be if you are swimming on a hot summer day?

90°F   50°F   150°F

9.
| 31 | 31 | 31 |
| +17 | +16 | +15 |

10. Jill has three skirts (navy, purple, and black). She has two pairs of shoes (white and red). How many different combinations of shoes and skirts can she make?

Exercise 30

Use this graph to answer
questions 1, 2, and 3.

Birds in the Park

cardinals					
blue jays					
sparrows					
crows					

⬜ = 2 birds

1. There were more _____ at
the park than any other kind of bird.

2. There were _____ cardinals at the
park.

3. There were _____ more crows than
sparrows at the park.

4. 2 + 2 + 2 + 2 = _____

4 + 4 = _____

2 × 4 = _____

5. Put these numbers in order from least to
greatest

61 21 41 51 31

_____ _____ _____ _____ _____

6. Circle the picture that shows $\frac{2}{3}$.

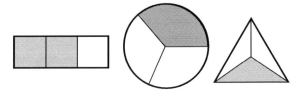

7. Make three different 3-digit numbers
with 5 in the tens place.

_____   _____   _____

8. How long is the train?

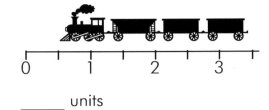

_____ units

9.
```
  182        182
+  16      +  10
```

10.
```
  48        48        48
 -18       -10        -8
```

Exercise 31

Use this graph to answer questions 1, 2, and 3.

Dogs at the Dog Show

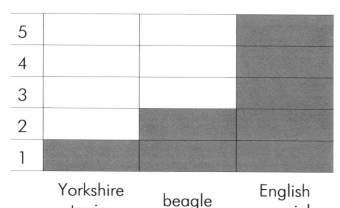

5			
4			
3			
2			
1			

Yorkshire terrier   beagle   English spaniel

1. There were less _____ than any other kind of dog. There was only _____ of this breed.

2. There were more _____ than any other dogs. There were _____ of this breed.

3. There was _____ more beagle at the show than Yorkshire Terriers.

. . . .

4. Count on by tens.

42, 52, ____, ____, ____

5. Complete the analogy.

10 : 20 :: 5 : ____

a. 25   **b.** 10   **c.** 20

. . . .

6. School started 15 minutes before the time shown on the clock. What time did school start?

____ : ____

. . . .

7. Finish the pattern.

90, 89, 88, ____, ____, ____

. . . .

8. Circle the one's digit in this number.

4 3 8

Write the number that is 10 more than 438.

_____

. . . .

9. Write the numeral for:

7000 + 30 + 7 + 500 = _____

. . . .

10.
| 24 | 24 | 24 |
| −4 | −5 | −6 |

Exercise 32

1. James had 76¢. He spent 30¢ on a ball and 25¢ on a pencil. How much money does he have left?

James has _____ ¢ left.

2. School gets out in a quarter of an hour after the time shown on the clock. What time will school get out?

_____ : _____

3. Make a chart to find out how much it costs to buy postcards.

cards	1	2	3	4
cost	25¢			

4. Circle the ten's digit in the number.

2,671

5. Circle the cube and put an ✖ on the sphere.

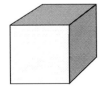

6. About how long does it take to take a shower?

10 minutes   10 hours   1 day

7. Fill in the missing numbers.

11, ___ , 15, ___ , ___ , 21, ___ , 25

8. Circle the odd numbers.

1 2 3 4 5 6 7 8 9

10 20 30 40 50 60 61

9.
```
  71          87
-28         -43
```

10. If you add 25¢ to this amount, how much money will you have?

_____ ¢

Exercise 33

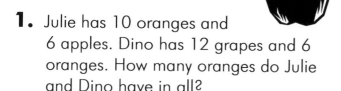

1. Julie has 10 oranges and 6 apples. Dino has 12 grapes and 6 oranges. How many oranges do Julie and Dino have in all?

_____ oranges

2. What time will it be in 25 minutes if it is 8:00 now? Draw the hands on the clock to show the correct time.

3. Show one way of making 46¢.

4. Show how to divide these apples equally among three people.

5. Count on by twos

10, 12, ____, ____, ____, ____

6. Insert >, =, or < to make this a true number sentence.

44 ◯ 38 + 6

7. Write two different number sentences that have a sum of 800.

_____

_____

8. Circle the drawing that shows 1/2 of a circle.

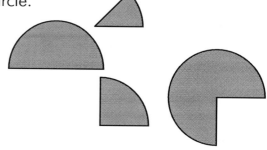

9.
```
  32        36
  25       −16
 +11
```

10. What fraction of the eggs are circled?

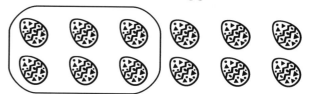

Exercise 34

1. Jack has 12 tennis balls. He can only fit 3 balls in one can. How many cans will Jack need to put away his tennis balls? Draw a picture.

_____ cans

2. What time is shown on the clock?

____ : ____

3. What is the perimeter of this triangle?

_____ centimeters

3 cm.
3 cm.
3 cm.

4. Draw a polygon with 6 sides. What is the name of this figure?

_____

5. Write the numerals for these words.

six hundred thirty-six _____

two hundred forty-five _____

one hundred twelve _____

6. Write fractions for the **unshaded** part of each drawing.

_____ , _____ , _____

7. How much money is shown?

_____ cents

8. Continue the pattern.

14, 12, 10, ____, ____, ____

The rule is _____

9.
$$57 - 12$$
$$43 - 31$$

10. Finish the fact family.

$6 \times 1 = $ ____

$6 \div $ ____ $ = $ ____

$1 \times $ ____ $ = 6$

$6 \div $ ____ $ = $ ____

Exercise 35

1. Miguel and his two friends each have six bananas. How many bananas do the three children have in all?

They have ____ bananas.

2. What time will it be in 45 minutes if it is 7:00 now? Draw the hands on the clock to show the time.

3. Complete the analogy.

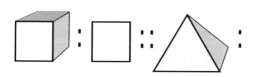

4. Count on by fives.

100, 105, ____, ____, ____

5. Insert >, =, or < to make this a true number sentence.

263 ◯ 236

6. 10 pennies = ____ nickels

15 pennies = ____ nickels

20 pennies = ____ dimes

7. Put the numbers in order from least to greatest.

4 44 54 34 14 24

____ ____ ____ ____ ____

8. Continue the pattern.

96, 95, 94, ____, ____, ____

9.
```
  14        88
  20       −80
 +34
```

10. Finish the fact family

2 × 3 = ____

6 ÷ ____ = ____

3 × ____ = ____

6 ÷ ____ = ____

Name _____

1. Misha's class earned 30 good behavior points in the morning. In the afternoon they lost 20 points. How many points did they have at the end of the day?

_____ points

If they continue this pattern, how many days will it take to earn 40 points?

_____ days

2. What time is shown on the clock?

____ : ____

3. Show how to make 28¢ with four coins.

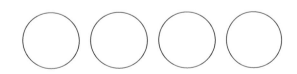

4. Complete the pattern.

20, 19, 18, ____, ____, ____

The rule is _____

5. Label each shape with the proper name.

_____   _____

6. Write three 2-digit even numbers.

_____ _____ _____

7. About how long is a new pencil?

1 cm   18 cm   180 cm

8. Insert >, =, or < to make this a true number sentence.

22 ◯ 20 + 2

9.
$$\begin{array}{r} 28 \\ -9 \\ \hline \end{array} \qquad \begin{array}{r} 9 \\ + \\ \hline 28 \end{array}$$

10. 16 − 2 = ____ + ____

16 + 2 = ____ + ____

Exercise 37

Name _____

1. There are 7 boys and 7 girls in Mrs. Jine's class. They are all wearing two shoes. How many shoes are there on the children in Mrs. Jine's class?

_____

2. Dinner is 45 minutes after the time shown on the clock. What time is dinner?

____ : ____

3.

_____ ¢

Show another way to make this amount of money using no more than 7 coins.

4. Complete the analogy.

88 : 880 :: 108 : ___

a. 801   **b.** 1090   **c.** 1080

5. Insert >, =, or < to make this a true number sentence.

44 ◯ 66 − 2

6. Complete the pattern.

60, 65, 70, ____, ____, ____

7. 1 dime + 1 nickel = _____ ¢

2 dimes + 1 nickel = _____ ¢

3 dimes + 1 nickel = _____ ¢

8. What part is shaded?

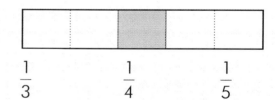

$\frac{1}{3}$ $\frac{1}{4}$ $\frac{1}{5}$

9. 19   9
      −9   +__
            19

10. What letter is the spinner most likely to land on?

_____

Exercise 38

Use this graph to answer
questions 1, 2, and 3.

Favorite Books

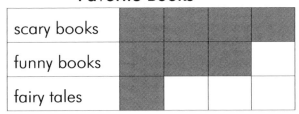

scary books				
funny books				
fairy tales				

▨ = 2 people's choice

1. What kind of book is the favorite?

_____

2. What kind is the least favorite book?

_____

3. How many more people like scary
books than fairy tales?

_____

· ·

4. How much money is shown?

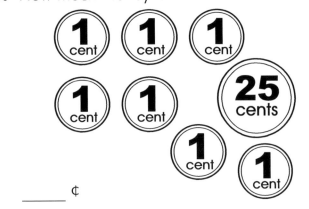

_____ ¢

5. Complete the analogy.

81 : 9 :: 100 : ___

a. 20   **b.** 5   **c.** 10

· ·

6. Finish the number sentences using the
fact family 9, 3, 27.

____ × ____ = 27

____ × ____ = ____

____ ÷ ____ = ____

____ ÷ ____ = ____

· ·

7. Circle the odd numbers.

88   99   110   111   112   113

· ·

8. What part is shaded?

$\frac{1}{4}$ $\frac{2}{4}$ $\frac{1}{3}$

· ·

9.   38   38
       +3   −10
      ____   ____

· ·

10. Complete the pattern .

1.0, 1.5, 2.0, _____, _____, _____

Exercise 39

1. Debbie, Joe, and Dan went to the library. They each checked out three books. How many books did they check out altogether?

_____ books

2. Recess is over 5 minutes after the time shown on the clock. What time will recess end?

____ : ____

3. You gave the clerk 75¢ and this is your change. How much was your purchase?

_____ ¢

4. Complete the analogy.

5. About how long is this pen?

_____ units

6. Round to the nearest ten.

77 _____   51 _____

22 _____   28 _____

7. Count on by tens.

31, 41, _____, _____, _____

8. Label each object with the correct name.

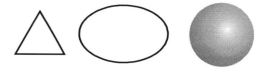

_____   _____   _____

9.
56	39	100
− 6	+ 6	− 5

10. Draw lines and shade the circle to show $\frac{3}{4}$.

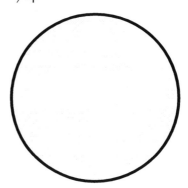

Exercise 40

1. Rafael had 25¢. He bought two pieces of candy for 8¢ each. How much money did Rafael have left?

_____ ¢

2. If it takes 10 minutes to set the table and Patrick starts at the time shown on the clock, when will he finish?

____ : ____

3. How much is 25¢ less than the money shown with these coins?

_____ ¢

4. Show how you could divide these packages evenly into eight groups.

5. Write a fraction for the **unshaded** part of each drawing.

____   ____   ____

6. Insert >, =, or < to make this a true number sentence.

100 ⬭ 100 – 2

7. Write the even numbers between 60 and 74.

_____

8. Put these in order of least to greatest.

28 18 8 38 58 48

___ ___ ___ ___ ___ ___

What is the pattern?

_____

9.
200   180
−10   +20

10. A box has these coins inside. Which one are you more likely to pull out if you stuck your hand inside without looking?

_____

Exercise 41

1. Maria has 80¢. What can she buy?

 = 55¢   = 50¢

 = 40¢   = 25¢

_____

_____

2. It is 9:10 now. Show what time will it be in 20 minutes.

____:____

3.

Show a different way of making this amount of money.

4. Write the number that comes before and the number that comes after each of these numbers.

____ 16 ____   ____ 49 ____

____ 87 ____   ____ 100 ____

5. quarter = _____ cents

3 quarters = _____ cents

6. About how much does a mouse weigh?

4 ounces   4 pounds   40 pounds

7. Count on by threes.

30, 33, ____, ____, ____

8. Draw a picture that shows $\frac{1}{3}$.

9. 14 − 7 = ____

140 − 70 = ____

10. Mindy is 2″ taller than Lisa but 3″ shorter than Jill. Draw a picture to show the girls in order from tallest to shortest.

Exercise 42

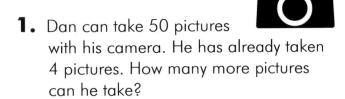

1. Dan can take 50 pictures with his camera. He has already taken 4 pictures. How many more pictures can he take?

___ pictures

2. It takes Britta 30 minutes to get ready for bed. If she has to turn out the light at 8:00 p.m., when does she have to start getting ready for bed?

___:___ p.m.

3. Write a mixed number for the **shaded** parts.

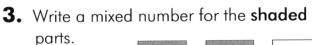

_____

4. You have these coins in your pocket. If you reach in and pull out two coins, what is the largest amount of money you can have?

_____ ¢

5. About how long is a spoon?

1 yard   1 foot   6 inches

6. Continue the pattern.

22, 33, 44, ____, ____, ____

7. What part of the submarines are circled?

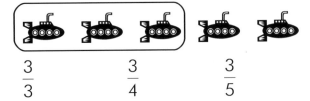

$\frac{3}{3}$ $\frac{3}{4}$ $\frac{3}{5}$

8. What two months come after October?

_____   _____

9.
```
  24        33
  23        26
+ 22      + 22
```

10.
```
  44        44        44
- 44      - 33      - 22
```

Exercise 43

1. Gary has 41 toy cars.  Jay has 60 toy cars. How many more toy cars does Jay have than Gary?

_____ cars

2. Lunch is in 2 hours and 20 minutes. What time is lunch?

_____ : _____

3. Complete the analogy.

4. Show how to make 45¢ with 4 coins.

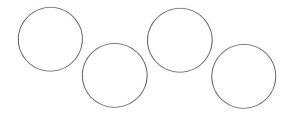

5. Insert >, =, or < to make this a true number sentence.

42 ⬭ 24 + 10

6. How many tens are in these numbers?

634   57   2,962

_____   _____   _____

7. About how long is this pencil?

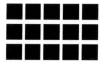

| 1' | 2' | 3' | 4' | 5' | 6' | 7' |

8. Put these numbers in order from greatest to least.

168   128   138   158   148

____ ____ ____ ____ ____

The pattern is _____

9. Which multiplication problem describes this array?

5 × 2   3 × 4   3 × 5

10.
140	120	110
− 40	−115	+160

Exercise 44

1. Alfredo has 31¢. Each package of gum costs 15¢. There are 5 pieces of gum in each package. How many packages of gum can he buy?

_____ packages

2. It takes 45 minutes to drive to the mall. If you leave at the time shown on the clock, when will you get to the mall?

____ : ____

3. Show how to make $1.35 using bills and coins.

4. Complete the analogy.

23 : 32 :: 45: ____

a. 55   **b.** 64   **c.** 54

5. Write the number for:
2 hundreds + 3 tens + 4 ones

_____

6. Insert >, =, or < to make this a true number sentence.

24 ◯ 20 + 4

7. What is the perimeter of the square?

P = _____ units

7 units

8. Finish the problems for the fact family 4, 6, 10.

4 + ____ = ____

____ + ____ = ____

10 − ____ = ____

____ − ____ = ____

9. Charla is making socks for her dogs. Help her figure out how many she has to make.

dogs	1	2	3	4
feet				

10.

29	307	31
+11	+111	−11

Exercise 45

1. Jerry has 6 blue cars and 2 red cars in his toy box. What is the probability he will pull out each color?

blue - —   red - —
     8   8

2. When the cats line up, how long a line do they make? _____ units

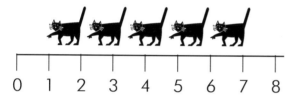

0   1   2   3   4   5   6   7   8

3. Round these numbers to the nearest hundred.

344 _____   374 _____

4. Show one way of making $1.75.

5. Insert >, =, or < to make this a true number sentence.

156 + 3 ⬭ 164 − 5

6. Draw hands on the clock to show half past one o'clock.

7. I have six ones. I have no tens. I have one hundred. What number am I?

_____

8. Draw a rectangle. Then draw a diagonal line from one corner to another corner.

9. 285   180
   + 3   −90

10. Complete the chart.

G	G + 10
3	13
15	
66	
210	

Exercise 46

Name _____

1. Kelly wants to divide these flowers evenly between herself and her two friends. How many flowers will each of them get?

_____ flowers each

2. Fill in the schedule.

Subject	length of class	time
reading	60 min.	9:00 -
math	45 min.	10:00 -
recess	15 min.	-11:00
writing	30 min.	11:00 -

3. What is 10 cents less than the amount of money shown on these coins?

_____ ¢

4. Complete the analogy.

3 : triangle :: 4 : _____

a. rectangle   **b.** pentagon   **c.** circle

5. Write a multiplication problem.

3 + 3 + 3 + 3 + 3 = ___ × ___

6. Put these numbers in order of greatest to least.

22 12 32 62 42 52

____ ____ ____ ____ ____ ____

7. Write the names of the shapes.

_____   _____

8. Insert >, =, or < to make this a true number sentence.

256 ◯ 156 + 10

9. Draw a picture that shows 4 × 3.

10. I am odd.
I am more than 10 and less than 20. What are all the possible numbers that I could be?

____ ____ ____ ____ ____

Exercise 47

Use this graph to answer questions 1, 2, and 3.

Favorite Months

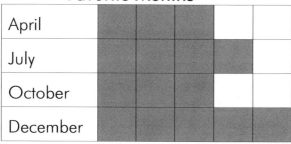

| April |
| July |
| October |
| December |

 = 2 people

1. How many people chose October as their favorite month? _____

2. How many more people chose December than chose October as their favorite month? _____

3. How many more people chose July than chose April as their favorite month?

_____

4. How much money is shown?

_____

5. Tricia starts piano practice at the time shown on the clock. She practices for 15 minutes. When does she stop?

____ : ____

6. Write the fraction to show the **shaded** part of each picture.

_____   _____   _____

Circle the largest fraction.

7. About how tall is your chair?

1 meter   10 meters   1 centimeter

8. Complete the table.

cups	1	2	3	4
pints	1/2	1		

9. 5 hundreds + 7 tens + 3 = _____

10. 180   180   180
       −160   −170   −180

Exercise 48

1. Meredith has 12 yellow pencils, 13 red pencils, and 16 silver pencils. How many pencils does she have altogether?

_____ pencils

2. Write fractions to show what part of the whole she has of each color.

yellow - ─   red - ─   silver - ─

3. Complete the analogy.

◄ : ◄◄ :: ► : ____

a. ▲   b. ►►| c. ►►

4. 1 week = ____ days

2 weeks = ____ days

3 weeks = ____ days

Kevin's birthday is in 3 weeks and 4 days. How many days until his birthday?

_____ days

5. Insert >, =, or < to make this a true number sentence.

36 ◯ 63 – 20

6. Show one way of making $1.00 with coins.

7. Write three 2-digit odd numbers.

____   ____   ____

8. Write the numeral for:

3 hundreds + 1 ten + 6 ones

_____

9.
```
 225        361
+167       +181
```

10. Draw a **pentagon**. Draw an **oval** to the left of the pentagon and a **triangle** to the right of the pentagon.

Exercise 49

1. Jay went to the zoo and saw 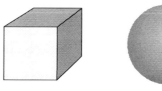 10 elephants. Six of the elephants had tusks. Write fractions and decimals to show how many elephants had tusks and how many did not have tusks.

with tusks $\dfrac{\quad}{10}$ = .6

without tusks $\dfrac{\quad}{10}$ = .___

2. Complete the analogy.

34 : 43 :: 67 : ____

a. 76   **b.** 77   **c.** 66

3. What time was it 5 minutes before the time shown on the clock?

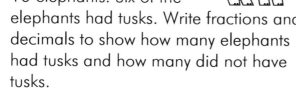

____ : ____

4. Show one way of making $1.75 with bills and coins.

5. Write the name of each shape.

_____   _____

6. Write two 4-digit even numbers.

_____   _____

7. I have 6 ones, 3 tens and 1 hundred. What number am I?

_____

8. Write these numbers in order of least to greatest.

120, 105, 115, 110, 125

____ ____ ____ ____ ____

9.
28	28	28
−10	− 9	−19

10. Draw an array to show 8 × 2 .

Exercise 50

1. Lorina had $10.50. Her mother gave her 25¢. She wants to buy a ring that costs $10.71. How much money will she have left after she buys the ring?

_____ ¢

2. Complete the analogy.

 : :: : ___

a. (clock)   b. (clock)   c. (clock)

3. 1 hour = 60 minutes

2 hours = ____ minutes

3 hours = ____ minutes

4 hours = ____ minutes

4. What is the area and the perimeter?

A = ____

P = ____

5. I have 1 one, 8 tens and 2 hundreds. What number am I?

_____

6. Label these triangles as either right, scalene or isosceles.

a. _____

b. _____

c. _____

7. Insert >, =, or < to make this a true number sentence.

646 ⟨ ⟩ 664

8. Write the fraction for the **shaded** portion of each object.

____   ____   ____

9. 48 + ____ = 52

10.
```
  2,312          5,816
 +7,416         -1,104
```

Exercise 51

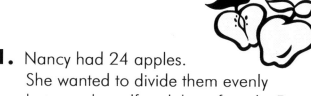

1. Nancy had 24 apples. She wanted to divide them evenly between herself and three friends. Draw a picture to show how many apples each of them got.

2. Draw a rectangle that is 4 squares tall and 6 squares long.

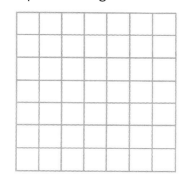

3. How many squares are inside the rectangle you drew?

_____ squares

4.
$$\begin{array}{r} \$.45 \\ +.45 \\ \hline \end{array} \qquad \begin{array}{r} \$ .75 \\ -.23 \\ \hline \end{array}$$

5. Insert >, =, or < to make this a true number sentence.

896 ◯ 869

6. Write the fraction of the **shaded** portion of each object.

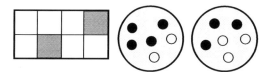

_____   _____   _____

7. About how long is a new pencil?

8 inches   8 centimeters   8 feet

8. Finish the problems for the fact family 5, 7, 35.

5 × ____ = ____

____ × ____ = ____

____ ÷ ____ = ____

____ ÷ ____ = ____

9.
$$\begin{array}{r} 423 \\ +618 \\ \hline \end{array} \qquad \begin{array}{r} 186 \\ -93 \\ \hline \end{array}$$

10. Write multiplication problems for these arrays.

_____   _____

Exercise 52

Name _____

1. Ms. Ray's class had a slipper party. There were 20 students, each wearing a pair of slippers. They put them in a big pile on the floor. How many slippers were in the pile?

_____ slippers

2. What time will it be 30 minutes after the time shown on the clock?

_____ : _____

3. Use a ruler to measure this line.

_____ inches

4. Kevin gets 25¢ every day for emptying the dishwasher. Make a chart to show how much he makes in a week.

day 1	25¢
day 2	
day 3	
day 4	$1.00
day 5	
day 6	
day 7	

5. Count on by fives.

25, 30, ___, ___, ___, ___

6. Finish the pattern.

18, 15, 12, 9, ___, ___, ___

7. If Derek is taller than 1 meter but shorter than 2 meters, how tall could he be?

a. 300cm.   b. 2 ½ m.   c. 1 ½ m.

8. Draw a picture to show $\frac{1}{4}$.

9.
$$\begin{array}{ccc} 518 & \$5.00 & 333 \\ +713 & +7.00 & -\ 81 \end{array}$$

10. What is the perimeter of this pentagon if each side is 5 units long?

P = ____

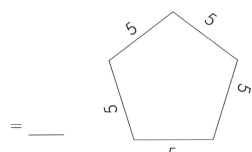

Exercise 53

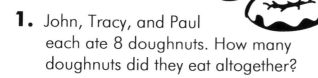

1. John, Tracy, and Paul each ate 8 doughnuts. How many doughnuts did they eat altogether?

_____ doughnuts

2. The temperature was 75° on Friday. It dropped 8° on Saturday. What was the temperature on Saturday? Shade the thermometer and write the temperature.

_____ °

3. Tell how many sides and vertices each of these polygons have.

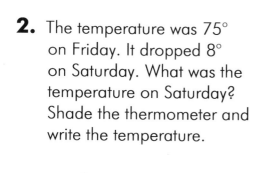

sides = _____   sides = _____

vertices = _____   vertices = _____

4. Complete the analogy.

17 : 51 :: 7 : _____

a. 3   **b.** 21   **c.** 17

5. How much money is shown?

_____ ¢

6. Insert >, =, or < to make this a true number sentence.

48 ◯ 480

7. Circle the drawing that shows $\frac{3}{4}$.

8. I have 2 hundreds, an even number of tens, and 9 ones. What numbers could I be?

_____ _____ _____ _____

9.

1,026	25	341
+3,133	51	− 19
	+13	

10. 2 × 10 = _____ = 5 × _____

Exercise 54

Use this graph to answer questions 1, 2, 3, and 4.

Favorite Movies

Finding Nemo	░	░				
Fox and Hound	░					
Lion King	░	░	░	░		
Aladdin	░	░	░	░	░	░

░ = two people

1. How many people like <u>The Fox and the Hound</u> best?

———

2. How many more people like <u>Aladdin</u> than like <u>Lion King</u>?

———

3. How many more people like the <u>Lion King</u> than like the <u>Fox and the Hound</u>?

———

4. Dora weighted 7 pounds 10 ounces when she was born. On her first birthday she weighted 20 pounds 14 ounces. How much weight did she gain in her first year?

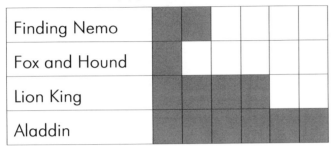

____ pounds ____ ounces

Name _____

5. Complete the analogy.

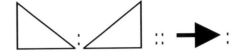

6. About how long is a new crayon?

4 centimeters   4 inches   4 feet

7. Complete the pattern.

63, 66, 69, ____, ____, ____

8. If this is half of the crayons in the box, how many crayons are in the box?

____ crayons in the box

9.
```
  141        126        12
 – 16       + 14        23
                       +45
```

10. Set A = {1, 3, 5, 7, 9, 11, 13, 15}

Set B = {3, 6, 9, 12, 15}

What numbers are in both set A and in set B?

———————————

Exercise 55

Name _____

1. Marissa has 16 red paper clips, 11 green paper clips and 25 gray paper clips. How many paper clips does she have in all?

_____ paper clips altogether

2. How many more red paper clips does she have than green paper clips?

_____ more red paper clips

3. What time will it be in 5 minutes?

____ : ____

4. Show one way of making 83¢.

5. Draw a figure that is congruent to this one.

6. Continue the pattern

16, 26, 36, ____, ____, ____

The rule is _____

7. Finish the fact family 9, 2, 18.

2 × ____ = ____

____ ÷ ____ = ____

____ × ____ = ____

____ ÷ ____ = ____

8. I am greater than 50 but less than 60. My digits are the same. What number am I?

_____

9.
253	526	7,050
−216	+ 9	−3,000

10. These 6 toy cars are in a toy box.

Is it possible to pull out the combination of 3 cars below? _____

Exercise 56

1. Felix has 10 pairs of white socks and 2 pairs of blue socks. If he reaches into his drawer without looking, which color of socks would he be more likely to pull out?

_____

2. Write the number that comes before and the number that comes after these numbers.

____ 49 ____

_____ 234 _____

_____ 1,592 _____

_____ 23,450 _____

3. What time will it be one hour and 15 minutes after the time shown on the clock?

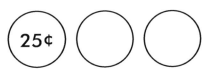

____ : ____

4. Complete the analogy.

45 : 450 :: 65 : ____

a. 655   **b.** 650   **c.** 70

5. Count on by tens.

12, 22, 32, ____, ____, ____

6. I have three coins that equal 35¢. One is a quarter.
What are the other two coins?

(25¢) ( ) ( )

7. Circle the 90° angle in the triangle.

8. Use the numbers 17, 8, and 9 to write four different number sentences.

17 – ____ = ____

____ – ____ = ____

____ + ____ = ____

____ + ____ = ____

9. 335   277
      −219   +133

10. On which letter is the spinner more likely to land on? _____

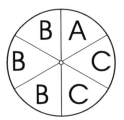

Exercise 57

Use this graph to answer
questions 1, 2, and 3.

Favorite Juices

● = 2 people

1. How many people chose apple juice as
their favorite?

_____

2. How many people chose orange juice
as their favorite?

_____

3. How many more people chose orange
juice than cranberry juice?

_____

4. What is the name of this solid figure?

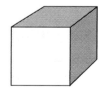

a. sphere   **b.** pyramid   **c.** cube

5. Add two coins to make 31¢.

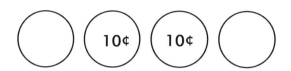

6. Count on by twos.

68, 70, ____, ____, ____, ____

7. Count on by tens.

21, ____, ____, ____, ____

8. ____¢ + 58¢ = 75¢

9.
44	18	1,800
+44	−9	−900

10. Write in the fractions to complete this
number line.

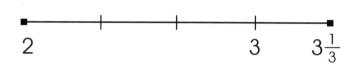

Exercise 58

1. If you were to spin a spinner ten times, which letter would the spinner land on the most?

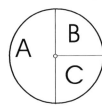

It would land most often on _____

because _____

2. Insert >, =, or < to make this a true number sentence.

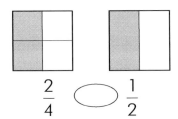

$\frac{2}{4}$ ◯ $\frac{1}{2}$

3. Brad is first in line to buy tickets for a movie. Kelly is last in line. Tom is behind Sam but in front of Kelly. Draw a picture to show how they are lined up.

4. Show how to make 96¢ using 8 coins.

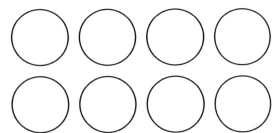

5. Complete the chart and give the rule.

x	rule
4	8
5	10
6	
10	
20	

6. $4 + 4 + 4 + 4 + 4 = $ __ $\times 4 = $ ___

7.
$$\begin{array}{r} 2,304 \\ -1,403 \\ \hline \end{array} \qquad \begin{array}{r} 2,304 \\ -1,303 \\ \hline \end{array} \qquad \begin{array}{r} 70 \\ 60 \\ +80 \\ \hline \end{array}$$

8. Which number sentences would give you the answer of 40?

41 − 1   30 + 5 + 4

20 + 20   65 − 20

9. $18 + 9 = 12 + $ ___

10.  = $5.00   = $6.00

How much will two baseballs and one kite cost?

$ _____

Exercise 59

Name _____

1. Julie has 20 red award ribbons, 5 blue ribbons and 2 white ribbons. Write fractions to show what part of all her ribbons are red, blue or white.

$$\frac{}{27} \qquad \frac{}{27} \qquad \frac{}{27}$$

red   blue   white

2. John left for the library at 2:00. The library is 20 minutes away. What time did John get there?

John got there at ____:____ .

3. = 15¢   = 10¢

How many balloons can you buy with 60¢? Draw a picture.

4. Write all the even numbers that are more than 20 and less than 30.

_____

If the sum of the digits in the number is ten, what is the number?

_____

5. Finish the pattern.

21, 26, 31, _____, _____, _____

6. Circle the triangle's right angle.

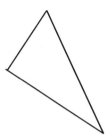

7. Shade the circles to make the number sentence true.

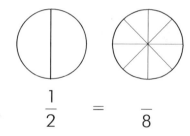

$$\frac{1}{2} \quad = \quad \frac{}{8}$$

8.
$$\begin{array}{r} 59 \\ -18 \\ \hline \end{array} \qquad \begin{array}{r} 10 \\ \times 8 \\ \hline \end{array} \qquad \begin{array}{r} 962 \\ +142 \\ \hline \end{array}$$

9. $18 - 9 = 9 + \underline{}$

10. Complete the analogy.

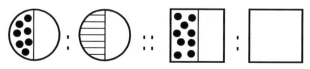

Exercise 60

Name _____

1. Write the numeral for:

seven hundred fifty-nine

_____

2. Write a number to make this number sentence true.

$493 < $ _____

3. What time was it 30 minutes ago if it is 8:00 now? Draw the hands on the clock and write the time.

_____ : _____

4. What is the perimeter of this triangle?

P = _____ units

5. Draw a circle around $\frac{5}{9}$ of the submarines.

6. Cut this candy bar so that 4 people get an equal piece. Write a fraction for the part each person gets.

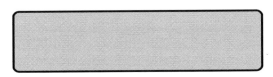

Each person gets _____.

7. 30¢ + 65¢ = 50¢ + _____

8.
```
  22        11        51
 -11        +         42
  __        __       +33
            22        __
```

9.
```
  244       122
 -122       +
  ___       ___
            244
```

10. I am odd.
I have four digits.
My thousands digit is less than 2.
My hundreds digit is 9.
My tens digit is 3.

What are all of the possible numbers that I could be?

_____ _____ _____

_____ _____

Exercise 61

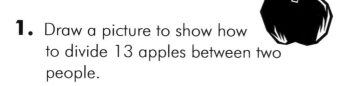

Name _____

1. Draw a picture to show how to divide 13 apples between two people.

Is this a fair share number? _____

2. Karen has 2 bicycles and 3 tricycles. How many wheels are on all of the tricycles and bicycles together?

There are _____ wheels.

3. Draw as many lines of symmetry as you can.

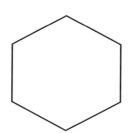

4. Dan is first in line and Mack is fourth in line. Jan is between Mack and Sally. Sally is behind Dan. Draw a picture to show all of these people and their places in line.

5. 1 year = _____ months

2 years = _____ months

6. Fill in the operation ($+$, $-$, $\times$, $\div$) to make these true number sentences.

(40 ◯ 10) ◯ 2 = 32

(6 ◯ 12) ◯ 3 = 15

7. Shade 3/4 of John's pizza.
Shade 5/8 of Jack's pizza.

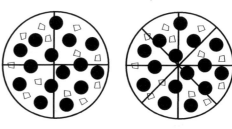

John (3/4)   Jack (5/8)

Who has the most pizza? _____

8. Finish the pattern.

59, 49, 39, _____, _____, _____

9. Insert $>$, $=$, or $<$ to make this a true number sentence.

$\dfrac{1}{2}$ ◯ $\dfrac{1}{5}$

10. About how long is the mouse?

0 1 2 3 4 5 6 7

____ units

Exercise 62

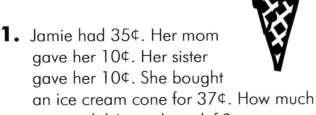

1. Jamie had 35¢. Her mom gave her 10¢. Her sister gave her 10¢. She bought an ice cream cone for 37¢. How much money did Jamie have left?

_____ ¢

2. Label the geometric shapes.

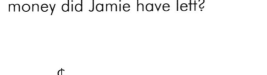

_____   _____

3. Kyle has to go to the store. The store is two miles away. How far will Kyle have to walk to go to the store and back?

Kyle will walk _____ miles.

4. Show how to make 30¢ using four coins.

5. Complete the analogy.

rectangle : 4 :: pentagon : _____

6. Fill in the missing numbers.

0, ½, _____, 1½, 2, _____, _____

7. What would the temperature be if it were 20° higher than the temperature shown on the thermometer?

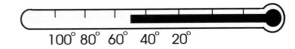
100° 80° 60° 40° 20°

_____ °

8. Complete the pattern.

68, 70, ____, ____, 76, ____

9.
62	73	9
−55	+18	×2

10. Dan owns four penguins named Mazey, Lucy, Tracy, and Lazy. Mazey is older than Lucy. Tracy is the youngest. Lazy is younger than Lucy. What is the name of the oldest penguin?

_____

Exercise 63

Use this graph to answer questions 1, 2, and 3.

Ways to Get to School

walk	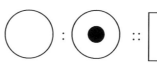		
bicycle			
bus			
car			

each picture = 2 students

1. How many students ride the bus? _____

2. How many students walk? _____

3. How many more students ride in a car than on a bus?

_____

4.   **Bus Schedule**

	mall	school	park
bus 1	10:00	10:15	10:35
bus 2	11:15	11:30	12:05

How long does it take to get from the mall to school? _____ minutes

Which bus makes the trip from school to the park in a shorter amount of time? _____

5. How many faces and vertices does this cube have?

faces = ____

vertices = ____

6. Complete the analogy.

$\bigcirc : \bigodot :: \square :$

7. 1 year = ____ months

1/2 year = ____ months

8. $4 \times 0 = 100 \times$ ____

9. Write an estimate and then solve this problem.

	estimate	solution
59		59
+16	+ ___	+16

10. Find a solution and then check your answer.

62	
−13	+13

Exercise 64

1. What is the length of this rectangle?

_____ units

0 1 2 3 4 5 6 7

2. Complete the analogy.

5 : 10 :: 10 : ____

a. 20   **b.** 100   **c.** 25

3. Circle the correct name for this figure.

rectangular prism
sphere
cone

4. Complete the table.

25	60	35	20	100
35	70			

5. 2 × 10 = 20 × ____

6. Derek's birthday is the 6th of June and Tina's birthday is the 6th of September. How many months between their birthdays?

_____ months

7. Which fraction shows the part of the group that are square turtles?

5/8   3/8   4/8

8.
82   30   16
−16   ×2   +66

9. Insert >, =, or < to make this a true number sentence.

199 ⬭ 200 − 2

10. What is the area of the inner rectangle?

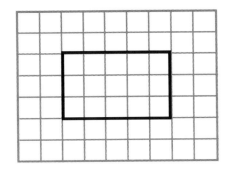

_____ square units

Exercise 65

Name _____

Use this calendar to answer questions 1, 2, and 3.

September

Sun	Mon	Tues	Wed	Thur	Fri	Sat
		1	2	3	4	5
6	7	8	9	10	11	12
13	14	15	16	17	18	19
20	21	22	23	24	25	26
27	28	29	30			

1. Stacy's play is on the third Friday of the month. What is the date?

_____

2. Her grandpa is coming 1 week and 1 day after the play. What day will he arrive?

_____

3. What date is the tenth day after the first Monday?

_____

4. How many sides and vertices does this figure have?

sides = ____

vertices = ____

5. Toby gets $5.00 allowance each week. If he saves it all, how much will he have in 6 weeks?

$____

6. Continue the pattern.

83, 73, 63, ____, ____, ____

7. Circle the shape that does not belong.

8. Write a mixed number for the shaded parts. _____

9. Write a multiplication problem for the array. Write another multiplication problem with the same product.

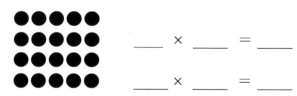

____ × ____ = ____

____ × ____ = ____

10. Write these fractions as decimals.

$\frac{5}{10}$ = .____ $\frac{9}{10}$ = .____

Exercise 66

1. There are six rabbits.
Three children each get
to hold the same number of rabbits.
Which picture shows how many rabbits
each child will get to hold?

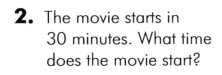

a.

b.

c.

2. The movie starts in
30 minutes. What time
does the movie start?

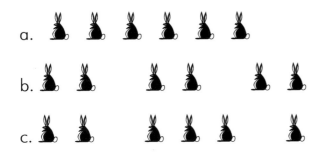

___:___

3. The movie is 3 hours long. What time
will the movie be over?

___:___

4. Complete the analogy.

50 : 100 :: 25 : _____

a. 75   **b.** 125   **c.** 50

5. Put these numbers in order from least
to greatest.

356 453 322 276

_____ _____ _____ _____

6. Matt's dog took a short nap. About
how long could he have slept?

1 hour   5 hours   20 hours

7. $20 \times 1 = 4 \times$ _____

8.
$$
\begin{array}{ccc}
283 & 345 & 100 \\
+164 & -172 & -44 \\
\hline
\end{array}
$$

9. Draw a picture to show $\dfrac{1}{4} < \dfrac{1}{2}$

10.  = 21¢

Draw the money you will need to buy
your dog 3 bones.

70

Exercise 67

1. Shade in the graph to correctly show the number of books these three boys have read?

Brad
Greg
Andrew

```
6 —
4 —
2 —
0 —
    | Brad | Greg | Andrew |
```

2.  = $350

If the camera is on sale for $125 off, what will the camera cost?

$ ____

3. Shade the drawing to show $\frac{2}{12}$.

4. About how long is this watch?

____ units

5. Finish the pattern.

686, 687, 688, _____, _____

6. $10 \times 0 = 15 \times$ ____

7. Write a mixed number to represent this picture. _____

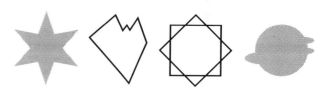

8.
| 268 | 315 | 7,009 |
| −84 | −60 | −1,005 |

9. Circle the symmetrical figures.

10. Lisa is taller than Joe. Joe is taller than Mandy. Kelly is taller than Joe and Lisa. Write their names from tallest to shortest.

1. _____   3. _____
   tallest

2. _____   4. _____
                   shortest

Name _____

1. Lisa is sitting in the third row of the movie theater. Her friend Joey is seven rows behind her. What row is Joey sitting in?

Joey is in row _____.

2. Each row of the theater has one more seat than the row before it. How many seats are in row 7? _____

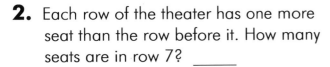

row	1	2	3	4	5	6	7
seats	19	20					

3. Circle the cylinder.

a.   b.   c.

4. What time was it 5 minutes before the time shown on the clock.

____ : ____

5. How many sides and vertices?

sides = ____

vertices = ____

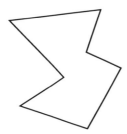

6. How many hundreds are in the number **982**?

There are _____ hundreds.

7.
$$422 - 391$$ $$2,200 - 1,900$$ $$\begin{array}{r} 74 \\ 33 \\ +\ 4 \\ \hline \end{array}$$

8. Complete the fact family.

$5 \times 3 = $ ____

____ $\times$ ____ $=$ ____

____ $\div$ ____ $=$ ____

____ $\div$ ____ $=$ ____

9. These coins total 78¢. Write the values on each coin.

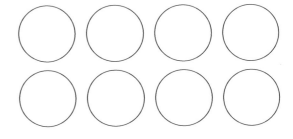

10. Circle the two congruent polygons.

a.   b.   c.

d.   e.   f.

Exercise 69

1. Make a bar graph to show the number of books each person read.

Julie ⌇⌇⌇⌇ ⌇⌇ Chris ⌇⌇⌇⌇ ⌇

Tom ⌇⌇⌇⌇ ⌇⌇ Hannah ⌇⌇⌇⌇

Number of Books Read

Julie					
Chris					
Tom					
Hannah					

2   4   6   8

2. How many wheels on 2 bikes, 2 wagons and 3 wheelbarrows?

_____ wheels

3. 6 + 6 = _____

60 + 60 = _____

600 + 600 = _____

4. Complete the analogy.

$$\frac{1}{4} : \frac{2}{4} :: \frac{1}{5} : \underline{\quad}$$

a. $\frac{2}{5}$ b. $\frac{1}{6}$ c. $\frac{5}{5}$

5. Draw a line between each object and its correct geometrical name.

cylinder

sphere

cube

6. Circle 1/4 of the helicopters.

7.

```
   7        15        150
 + ___     - ___     - ___
  15         7         70
```

8. 2 × 2 = 1 × _____

9. Insert >, =, or < to make this a true number sentence.

942 ◯ 294 + 500

10. About how much does a coat weigh?

1 ounce   1 pound   10 pounds

Exercise 70

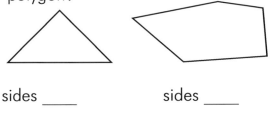

1. Jill practiced the piano 12 hours this week and 11 hours last week. About how many hours did she practice for both weeks?

about **10** hours   **20** hours   **30** hours

2. Heidi starts practicing ballet at the time shown on the clock. She practices for 1 hour and 5 minutes. When does she finish?

_____:_____

3. The money totals $5.65 Write the amounts on each coin and bill.

4. Tina reads 5 more pages a day than she did the day before. How many pages will she read on the fifth day?

day	1	2	3	4	5
pages	10				

5. How many sides and vertices for each polygon?

sides ____   sides ____

vertices ____   vertices ____

6. Circle 1/4 of the bags of money.

7. If each bag has $10 in it, how much money is in all the bags?

$ _____

8. Write the number that is 1,000 more than each of these numbers.

69 _____   23,571 _____

190 _____   2,589 _____

9.
```
  33        268       4,050
+18        −88      +2,500
____       ____      _____
```

10. Jake ate 2/8 of his pizza for lunch and 3/8 for dinner. How much of the whole pizza did he eat?   _____

Answers

Exercise 1, pg. 5
1. 6
2. 40¢
3. 20, 30
   rule: add 5
4. 17
5. even
6. 6 units
7. 9:00
8. 2
9. 367
10. second clock should be circled

Exercise 2, pg. 6
1. 2 books
2. 3:00
3. shade half
4. 9, 11, 13
   rule: add 2
5. All sides are equal and all angles are 90°.
6. ◖
7. 17   262
8. 6   60
9. 2
10. 2 + 3 = 5   5 - 3 = 2
    3 + 2 = 5   5 - 2 = 3

Exercise 3, pg. 7
1. 6:00
2. shade half
3. 17, 19, 21
4. 2, 4, 6
5. ●●▲
6. 3 cups
7. 16¢
8. 12   14
9. 16   18
10. 20¢

Exercise 4, pg. 8
1. 3
2. four; 4
3. 32¢
4. 8
5. 10:00
6. rectangle divided into four equal parts
7. 18   14   32
8. 4   20   30
9. 1 lb
10. 18, 20, 22
    rule: add 2

Exercise 5, pg. 9
1. 5
2. 4
3. yellow
4. c. feet
5. 5:00
6. 4   3
7. 7   17
8. ✳
9. rectangle
10. b. first

Exercise 6, pg. 10
1. blue
2. quarter; 50¢
3. 5
4. 7 + 3 = 10   10 - 3 = 7
   3 + 7 = 10   10 - 7 = 3
5. 11, 13, 15
6. 2
7. color 5 faces   1/2 or 5/10
8. circle the fifth cake
9. even
10. c. 6

Exercise 7, pg. 11
1. 9
2. 9:30
3. a. afternoon
4. 50, 55, 60
5. 6 ounces
6. 4, 5, 6, 8, 9, 10
7. 25¢
8. 15   15
9. 11 - 5
10. 1 meter

Exercise 8, pg. 12
1. 5, 5
2. 1:30
3. divide into 4 equal parts
4. April
5. 28
6. 3
7. triangle
8. 19   17   170
9. answers will vary
10. 2

Exercise 9, pg. 13
1. 3
2. 2
3. 2:30
4. 4
5. 1   2
6. >
7. 89, 88, 87
   rule: subtract 1
8. 8
9. 4
10. 12   13   14   15

Exercise 10, pg. 14
1. 31¢
2. James   4¢
3. 25
4. 10   20   30
5. 9, 8, 7, 6
6. 6 airplanes in each group
7. 30, 35
8. circle first, third and sixth cats
9. 6   6
10. 4 + 6

Exercise 11, pg. 15
1. 12
2. brown
3. b. months
4. 5   10   15
5. 5   11
6. 2, 4, 6
7. 4:00
8. shade half
9. 4   4
10. 9   15   25

Exercise 12, pg. 16
1. 8   8
2. 12:30
3. a. opposite direction and color
4. rectangle
5. 7 feet
6. $6 + 2 = 8$ $8 - 2 = 6$
   $2 + 6 = 8$ $8 - 6 = 2$
7. 60   30
8. 2   4   6
9. 13   13
10. 8   8   15

Exercise 13, pg. 17
1. 8
2. 1 hour and 10 minutes
3. 40¢
4. A square has four equal sides.
5. 4
6. $=$
7. 6   17
8. 1   50¢
9. 12   22
10. 6   7   8
    Answers will vary.

Exercise 14, pg. 18
1. 40¢
2. clock showing 8:15
3. a. half
4. 25   50   75
5. $<$
6. 90, 91, 92
    rule: add 1
7. 5, 7, 9, 11
    $11 + 9 = 20$ $8 + 12 = 20$
8. $\frac{1}{2} = \frac{2}{4}$
9. 21   19   20
10. 60

Exercise 15, pg. 19
1. 5
2. b. 3
3. clock showing 3:30
4. 7 inches
5. circle the seventh apple
6. 40, 45, 50
    rule: add 5
7. color half $1/2 = 3/6$
8. 25   30   35
9. 18
10. 6 6 7 7

Exercise 16, pg. 20
1. yes
2. 10 tens = 100   40 tens = 400
    70 tens = 700
3. 26
4. $>$
5. $7 + 4 = 11$ $11 - 7 = 4$
   $4 + 7 = 11$ $11 - 4 = 7$
6. answers will vary
7. 17, 19 $17 + 19 = 36$
8. circle the triangle
9. $8 + 2$
10. $10¢ + 10¢ + 5¢$

Exercise 17. pg. 21
1. 5
2. 5:15
3. c. tomorrow
4. 44, 45, 46, 48, 49
5. October
6. 25¢
7. 2, 12, 20 $20-2 = 18$
8. 8   16
9. circle the square
10. 8 9 10

Exercise 18, pg. 22
1. 5
2. tomato
3. a. Monday
4. 40, 50, 60, 70
5. circle the picture on the right
    that shows one shaded square
    out of 6 squares
6. $6 + 8 = 14$ $8 + 6 = 14$
   $14 - 6 = 8$ $14 - 8 = 6$
7. 6   633
8. 16¢
9. 22
10. $16 - 6$

Exercise 19, pg. 23
1. 24
2. 4:45; 15 minutes
3. a. pair
4. 1, 3, 5, 7
5. $<$
6. circle 4 cones
7. 32¢
8. 12, 15, 18
9. $4 + 8 = 12$ $12 - 4 = 8$
   $8 + 4 = 12$ $12 - 8 = 4$
10. 16   15   14

Exercise 20, pg. 24
1. Tracy, Randy, Pat
2. 45 minutes; 10:00
3. shade 3 parts
4. 63, 73, 83, 93
5. 4 months
6. 86, 85, 84
7. 12¢
8. 76
9. 9,632
10. 24 23 22

Exercise 21, pg. 25
1. 5
2. 19th
3. 7 days
4. 5 days
5. ▲■◆◆
6. 15, 25, 35, 45, 55
7.

8. circle 4 snakes $\frac{1}{3} = \frac{4}{12}$
9. 21   21
10. cup

Exercise 22, pg. 26
1. 5 loaves   40 while slices
2. clock hands should show 3:30
3. 1,248
4. 35, 40, 45
5. 7 14 12
6. 11, 13, 15
    rule: add 2
7. circle the paint can
8. 27¢
9. 20   38
10. 21   20   19

Exercise 23, pg. 27
1. 9 fish
2. 5 units
3. b. 6:00
4. 61, 51, 41
5. 32¢
6. 9, 11, 13   sum = 33
7. pentagon   triangle
8. circle 2 trucks $\frac{1}{5} = \frac{2}{10}$
9. $13 + 6$
10. 60   66

Exercise 24, pg. 28
1. 8
2. 2
3. 6
4. 55, 65, 75
5. drawing should be mirror image of what is drawn
6. >
7. 2, 3   II, III
8. 15 minutes
9. 12   12
10. 40   39   38

Exercise 25, pg. 29
1. 14   7
2. 4
3. clock hands should show 3:45
4. 6 units
5. triangle   3
6. 197, 195
   rule: subtract 1
7. 12, 14, 16, 18
8. shade one star
9. 8, 8, 2
10. 10 people

Exercise 26, pg. 30
1. 4 cupcakes
2. 1:25
3. a. 10
4. 19, 17, 15, 13, 11
5. 4   14   40
6. 30 minutes
7. 45¢
   1 - 25¢ and 4 - 5¢
8. draw lines of symmetry for each polygon
9. 20   10   30
10. 21 34 18 57

Exercise 27, pg. 31
1. 20 children; 29 children
2. 5:30
3. a. 8
4. 35, 45, 55, 65
5. 5/6   1/3   2/4
6. 7 + 8 = 15   8 + 7 = 15
   15 - 8 = 7   15 - 7 = 8
7. 45¢
8. >
9. 12   12
10. 32   31   30

Exercise 28, pg. 32
1. 12   6
2. clock showing 12:45
3. shade circles to show
   1/2   3/6   5/10
4. 215   220   225   230   235
5. 7 circles, 9 circles
6. 10 - even   15 - odd
   25 - odd   30 - even
7. 2,162
8. June
9. 54   55   155
10. 70 + 30   60 + 40
    10 + 90

Exercise 29, pg. 33
1. 5 brownies
2. 10:05
3. small black triangle
4. 40, 45, 50
5. shade 4 cats
6. 196, 195, 194
7. circle the fifth can in the second row
8. 90° F
9. 48   47   46
10. 6 combinations
    NW NR PW PR BW BR

Exercise 30, pg. 34
1. crows
2. 8
3. 4
4. 8   8   8
5. 21, 31, 41, 51, 61
6. circle first picture
7. any 3-digit number with 5 tens
8. 3 units
9. 198   192
10. 30   38   40

Exercise 31, pg. 35
1. Yorkshire terrier, 1
2. English spaniel, 5
3. 1
4. 62, 72, 82
5. b. 10
6. 8:00
7. 87, 86, 85
8. circle 8   448
9. 7,537
10. 20   19   18

Exercise 32, pg. 36
1. 21¢
2. 2:15
3. 50¢ 75¢ $1.00
4. 7
5. circle the cube; X on the sphere
6. 10 minutes
7. 13, 17, 19, 23
8. 1 3 5 7 9 61
9. 43   44
10. 25¢

Exercise 33, pg. 37
1. 16 oranges
2. clock showing 8:25
3. answers will vary
4. 3 apples in each group
5. 14 16 18 20
6. =
7. answers will vary
8. circle the semi-circle
9. 68, 20
10. 6/12 or 1/2

Exercise 34, pg. 38
1. 4 cans
2. 3:35
3. 9 cm.
4. drawing of a 6-sided figure hexagon
5. 636   245   112
6. 2/4   2/6   1/3
7. 42¢
8. 8, 6, 4
   rule: subtract 2
9. 45, 12
10. 6 x 1 = 6   1 x 6 = 6
    6 ÷ 1 = 6   6 ÷ 1 = 6

Exercise 35, pg. 39
1. 18 cherries
2. hands on the clock show 7:45
3. triangle
4. 110, 115, 120
5. >
6. 2   3   2
7. 4, 14, 24, 34, 44, 54
8. 93, 92, 91
9. 68, 8
10. 2 x 3 = 6   3 x 2 = 6
    6 ÷ 2 = 3   6 ÷ 3 = 2

Exercise 36, pg. 40
1. 10 points, 4 days
2. 9:45
3. 1 - 25¢ and 3 - 1¢
4. 17, 16, 15
   rule: subtract 1
5. rectangle   pentagon
6. answers will vary
7. 18 cm.
8. =
9. 19   19
10. answers will vary, sum should
    be 14 and 18

Exercise 37, pg. 41
1. 28 shoes
2. 7:00
3. 50¢, answers will vary
4. c. 1080
5. <
6. 75, 80, 85
7. 15¢   25¢   35¢
8. 1/5
9. 10, 10
10. G

Exercise 38, pg. 42
1. scary books
2. fairy tales
3. 6
4. 32¢
5. c. 10
6. $9 \times 3 = 27$ $27 \div 3 = 9$
   $3 \times 9 = 27$ $27 \div 9 = 3$
7. 99, 111, 113
8. 1/3
9. 41   28
10. 2.5 3.0 3.5

Exercise 39, pg. 43
1. 9 books
2. 2:50
3. 30¢
4. small hexagon with a diagonal
   in the opposite direction
5. 5 units
6. 80, 20, 50, 30
7. 51, 61, 71
8. triangle, oval, sphere
9. 50   45   95
10. draw lines and shade 3/4

Exercise 40, pg. 44
1. 9¢
2. 5:10
3. 75¢
4. groups of 3
5. 5/8   1/4   3/4
6. >
7. 62 64 66 68 70 72
8. 8, 18, 28, 38, 48, 58; add 10
9. 190   200
10. quarter

Exercise 41, pg. 45
1. answers will vary
2. clock showing 9:30
3. answers will vary
4. 15, 16, 17   48, 49 50
   86, 87, 88   99, 100, 101
5. 25¢, 75¢
6. 4 oz.
7. 36, 39, 42
8. answers vary
9. 7   70
10. Jill   Mindy   Lisa

Exercise 42, pg. 46
1. 46 pictures
2. 7:30 p.m.
3. $2\frac{1}{3}$
4. 35¢
5. 6 in.
6. 55 66 77
7. 3/5
8. November   December
9. 69   81
10. 0   11   22

Exercise 43, pg. 47
1. 19 cars
2. 12:20 p.m.
3. square with a dark circle inside
4. 1- 25¢ 2- 5¢ 1- 10¢
5. >
6. 3 5 6
7. 5 units
8. 168, 158, 148, 138, 128
   pattern - subtract 10
9. 3×5
10. 120   5   270

Exercise 44, pg. 48
1. 2 packages
2. 6:15
3. answers will vary
4. c. 54
5. 234
6. =
7. 28 units
8. $4 + 6 = 10$ $10 - 4 = 6$
   $6 + 4 = 10$ $10 - 6 = 4$
9. 4 8 12 16
10. 40   418   20

Exercise 45, pg. 49
1. blue - 6/8   red - 2/8
2. 6 units
3. 300   400
4. answers will vary
5. =
6. clock should show 1:30
7. 106
8. drawing of an rectangle with a
   diagonal
9. 288, 90
10. 13   25   76   220

Exercise 46, pg. 50
1. 7 flowers each
2. reading   9:00-10:00
   math   10:00-10:45
   recess   10:45-11:00
   writing   11:00-11:30
3. 65¢
4. a. rectangle
5. 3 x 5
6. 62, 52, 42, 32, 22, 12
7. triangle   square
8. >
9. 4 rows, 3 objects in each row
10. 11, 13, 15, 17,19

Exercise 47, pg. 51
1. 6
2. 4
3. 2
4. $1.20
5. 2:50
6. 2/4   1/5   2/6   circle 2/4
7. 1 meter
8. $1\frac{1}{2}$ 2
9. 573
10. 20   10   0

Exercise 48, pg. 52

1. 41 pencils
2. yellow - 12/41   red - 13/41
   silver - 16/41
3. c. ▸▸
4. 7 14 21; 25
5. <
6. answers will vary
7. answers will vary
8. 316
9. 392   542
10. ⬭ ⬠ △

Exercise 49, pg. 53

1. tusks - 6/10 = .6
   without tusks - 4/10 = .4
2. a. 76
3. 9:30
4. answers will vary
5. cube   sphere
6. answers will vary
7. 136
8. 105, 110, 115, 120, 125
9. 18   19   9
10. drawing of 8 rows of 2 objects

Exercise 50, pg. 54

1. 4¢
2. a. 🕐
3. 120 180 240
4. A = 20   P = 18
5. 281
6. a. right   b. isosceles,
   c. scalene
7. <
8. 1/4   4/13   5/8
9. 4
10. 9,728   4,712

Exercise 51, pg. 59

1. 6 apples in each group
2. 4x6 rectangle
3. 24 squares
4. $.90 $.52
5. >
6. 2/8   4/6   3/6
7. 8 inches
8. 5 × 7 = 35   35 ÷ 7 = 5
   7 × 5 = 35   35 ÷ 5 = 7
9. 1041   93
10. 4x5   2x10

Exercise 52, pg. 56

1. 40 slippers
2. 10:05
3. 2 ½ inches
4. 25¢ 50¢ 75¢ $1.00 $1.25
   $1.50 $1.75
5. 35, 40, 45, 50
6. 6, 3, 0
7. b. 2 ½ m.
8. picture showing 1/4
9. 1231 $12.00 252
10. 25 units

Exercise 53, pg. 57

1. 24 doughnuts
2. 67°
3. 7, 7; 5, 5
4. b. 21
5. 111¢
6. <
7. circle the star
8. 209, 229, 249, 269, 289
9. 4,159   89   322
10. 20;   4

Exercise 54, pg. 58

1. 2
2. 4
3. 6
4. 13 lb. 4 oz.
5. ⬅
6. 4 inches
7. 72   75   78
8. 16 crayons
9. 125   140   80
10. 3, 9, 15

Exercise 55, pg. 59

1. 52
2. 5
3. 1:50
4. answers will vary
5. drawing should be the same as
   the one given
6. 46   56   66
   rule: add 10
7. 2 × 9 = 18   9 × 2 = 18
   18 ÷ 2 = 9   18 ÷ 9 = 2
8. 55
9. 37   535   4,050
10. no

Exercise 56, pg. 60

1. white
2. 48   49   50
   233   234   236
   1,591   1,592   1,593
   23,499   23,450   23,451
3. 12:15
4. b. 650
5. 42, 52, 62
6. 2 - 5¢
7. 90° angle should be circled
8. 17 - 9 = 8   8 + 9 = 17
   17 - 8 = 9   9 + 8 = 17
9. 116   410
10. B

Exercise 57, pg. 61

1. 4
2. 12
3. 4
4. c. cube
5. 1 - 10¢   1 - 1¢
6. 72   74   76   78
7. 31, 41, 51, 61
8. 17¢
9. 88   9   900
10. 2 ⅓   2 ⅔

Exercise 58, pg. 62

1. A, biggest area of the spinner
2. =
3. Brad, Sam, Tom, Kelly
4. 2-25¢ 4-10¢ 1-5¢ 1-1¢
5. 12   20   40
   rule: multiply by 2
6. 5 x 4 = 20
7. 901   1001   210
8. 41 - 1 and 20 + 20
9. 15
10. $17.00

Exercise 59, pg. 63

1. red - 20/27   blue - 5/27
   white - 2/27
2. 2:20
3. answers will vary
4. 22, 24, 26, 28; 28
5. 36, 41, 46
6. circle the right triangle
7. shade ½ of each drawing $\frac{1}{2} = \frac{4}{8}$
8. 41   80   1,104
9. 0
10. same pattern as in the square

Exercise 60, pg. 64
1. 759
2. anything greater than 493.
3. clock hands showing 7:30
4. 41
5. circle 5 submarines
6. draw lines to divide into quarters; 1/4
7. 45¢
8. 11, 11, 126
9. 122   122
10. 1,931, 1,933, 1,935, 1,937, 1,939

Exercise 61, pg. 65
1. 6 apples in 2 groups; 1 left over; no
2. 13 wheels
3. 6 lines of symmetry
4. Dan, Sally, Jan, Mack
5. 12   24
6. $(40 - 10) + 2 = 32$
   $(6 + 12) - 3 = 15$
7. pizzas shaded to show 3/4 and 5/8   John
8. 29, 19, 9
9. >
10. 5 units

Exercise 62, pg. 66
1. 18¢
2. hexagon, prism
3. 4 miles
4. 10¢   10¢   5¢   5¢
5. 5
6. 1 $2\frac{1}{2}$ 3
7. 70°
8. 72, 74, 78
9. 7   91   18
10. Mazey

Exercise 63, pg. 67
1. 2
2. 4
3. 4
4. 15 minutes; bus 1
5. faces = 6   vertices = 8
6. rectangle with black circle in it
7. 12 months; 6 months
8. 0
9. $60 + 20 = 80$ 75
10. 49, $49 + 13 = 62$

Exercise 64, pg. 68
1. 4
2. a. 20
3. rectangular prism
4. 45   30   110
5. 1
6. 3 months
7. 3/8
8. 66   60   82
9. >
10. 15 square units

Exercise 65, pg. 69
1. Sept. 18th
2. Sept 26th
3. Sept. 17th
4. 10, 10
5. $30
6. 53, 43, 33
7. cylinder
8. $3\frac{1}{4}$
9. 4 x 5; any equation that has a product of 20
10. .5   .9

Exercise 66, pg. 70
1. b. 3 groups of 2
2. 3:35
3. 6:35
4. c. 50
5. 276, 322, 356, 453
6. 1 hour
7. 5
8. 447   173   56
9. answers will vary
10. any combination of coins that equal 63 cents

Exercise 67, pg. 71
1. graph shaded correctly
   Brad = 6   Greg = 3
   Andrew = 4
2. $225
3. shade 2 pencils
4. 7 units
5. 689, 690
6. 0
7. $4\frac{3}{4}$
8. 184   255   6004
9. the first and third figures
10. Kelly, Lisa, Joe, Mandy

Exercise 68, pg. 72
1. 10
2. 21   22   23   24   25
3. a. cup
4. 9:40
5. 7 sides   7 vertices
6. 9
7. 31   300   111
8. 5 x 3 = 15   15 ÷ 5 = 3
   3 x 5 = 15   15 ÷ 3 = 5
9. 2-25¢   2-10¢   1-5¢   3-1¢
10. a. and e.

Exercise 69, pg. 73
1. correctly shaded graph
   Julie = 7   Tom = 7
   Chris = 6   Hannah = 4
2. 15 wheels
3. 12   120   1200
4. a. $\frac{2}{5}$
5. cube, cylinder, sphere
6. circle 3 helicopters
7. 8   8   80
8. 4
9. >
10. 1 pound

Exercise 70, pg. 74
1. about 20 hours
2. 9:30
3. 1-$1   2-25¢   3-5¢
4. 15   20   25   30
5. 3, 3   5, 5
6. circle 2 bags
7. $80
8. 1,069   24,572
   1,190   3,589
9. 51   180   6,550
10. 5/8

Common Core State Standards Alignment Sheet
Math Warm-Ups (Grade 2)

All lessons in this book align to the following standards.

Grade Level	Common Core State Standards in Math
Grade 2	2.OA.A Represent and solve problems involving addition and subtraction. 2.OA.B Add and subtract within 20. 2.OA.C Work with equal groups of objects to gain foundations for multiplication. 2.NBT.A Understand place value. 2.NBT.B Use place value understanding and properties of operations to add and subtract. 2.MD.A Measure and estimate lengths in standard units. 2.MD.C Work with time and money. 2.G.A Reason with shapes and their attributes.
Grade 3	3.OA.A Represent and solve problems involving multiplication and division. 3.NF.A Develop understanding of fractions as numbers. 3.MD.A Solve problems involving measurement and estimation. 3.MD.C Geometric measurement: understand concepts of area and relate area to multiplication and to addition. 3.G.A Reason with shapes and their attributes.

Key:
OA = Operations & Algebraic Thinking; NBT = Number & Operations in Base Ten; NF = Number & Operations--Fractions; MD = Measurement & Data; G = Geometry